the stars in your eyes

Aarushi Bhargava

BookLeaf Publishing

Presentation by *BookLeaf Publishing*

Web: www.bookleafpub.com

E-mail: info@bookleafpub.com

ISBN: 978-93-5744-941-0

First edition 2022

DEDICATION

to those who can't yet see

the stars in their eyes

ACKNOWLEDGEMENT

Thank you to the amazing people in my life who convinced me to jump into the magical world of poetry.

PREFACE

"Dwell on the beauty of life. Watch the stars, and see yourself running with them."

-    Marcus Aurelius,

coyote

i used to walk past the coyotes den each
morning.
i waited, knowing the eyes that peered across
my back
Scanned my face
Watched my eyes,
i walked past the coyotes den each morning
Wondering if i would make it past
Wondering if they would hurt me
wishing that they could

i used to walk past the coyotes den each
morning,
Knowing that i might not make it past

A bridge over a raging river,
But a path unfinished.

i used to wonder as i tread the path
Would i fall, into the dark abyss?
Could i fall into the dark abyss,

Could i feel the pain surround my skin
Could i feel it pull the blood out of the veins
And leave its scars on my wrists.

i used to walk past the coyotes den each
morning,
Feeling the eyes,
Hoping to find myself floating in the darkness.

heart racing

Why wont You stop?
Why wont You stop screaming your profanity
at me?
Why wont You stop whispering your wounds in
my ears?

Why wont You rest your voice and heal your
hands?
Why wont You collect the pieces of your heart
one by one and fit the pieces back together?

tape & glue

No one was there, so i told myself
That id fix my heart
With tape and glue
i told myself that id put together each of the
tiny shards of red
And make my heart whole again

When you weren't there, i held my heart
together with tape & glue

Only the glue took too long to dry

And the tape was just never sticky enough

i tried

Sometimes i tried
To put my heart in your hands
To ask you to fill the missing pieces

But you pushed me away
You pushed me down
And dissolved into the shadows

night

One night in the wisps of darkness you
whispered to me -

When my eyes fill up with tears
And my lungs drown in water
Do you see the pain that pierces my soul
Do you see me close my eyes, to hide the hurt
Do you see me?

Do
You
See
Me?

Your eyes are open, but

Do you watch the small fissures open in my
heart
Do you watch my cheeks stain with blue
Do you watch me hide in the darkness

My arms wrapped around my chest
Holding myself in your grasp

tear filled

i used to wonder if when i cried
You would listen for the drop of my tears as
they fell

i used to wonder if when the pain became
unbearable
Would you see the clouds as they gathered
above my soul

Would you hear the clap of thunder
And the roar of lightning

As it
    Crashed down
        On me

When i was so filled with cracks and couldn't
hold myself together,
Could you see me shatter?

Would you be careful

To step over the shards of glass
As to not hurt me more?

Would you hold my heart in your hands
And keep it safe?

happy

They told me i used to be happy

They told me i was happy

They told me to be happy

Happy

happy

...happy

not the end, but the

start

;

drive

i drove towards the sun
To its everlasting warmth
And its blinding rays

And then put on music so loud to drown out
your words
To silence you

...To silence me

...To silence my *pain*

sunrise

I watched the sun rise above the horizon
Touching the earth with its fingers
Bringing its glow to me and you

I watched it cover your body
And glint through the hazel of your eyes

But you couldn't feel its warmth
You couldn't feel its glow

You couldn't see how it made your skin sparkle
Like a million tiny gems

wish

I stood alone
And looked up at the skies
And wished for a sign from the angels above
me
Wished for a sign that there was a reason that
I was still here

rain

I watched as the sky turned grey
And sank to my knees and felt each drop of
water fall upon my skin and bring it back to life

I heard the stars whisper in my ears as the
cosmos brushed away the tears from my skin
And held each part of my body together
As it fit each piece back where it belonged
As It peeled away
The tape and glue
And stitched my heart back into one
With gentle care it caressed my cheek

And told me to stand up again
To feel the earth beneath my feet
To feel the warmth of the breath in my lungs
To open my eyes

And *see* again

stardust

What if I could tell you that your heart is part of
a star
That the blood in your veins carries iron from
the moon
That the ringing in our ears is truly the
twinkling of the stars
And dreams are simply our nightly travels up
into the cosmos

If only you would hear when i told you
That you are made from the dust that falls from
the stars and the scars on your skin
are simply from comets shooting across the
sky and colliding with your soul

What if I could show you that the
constellations in the sky are the bonds
between the stars
That hold our lives together

What if the clusters of stars in the sky reflect
our hearts as they join together in a fiery
passion

But what if back down here, held down by
gravity, where the skies are covered with
smoke
And the light of the stars is only a speck of
dust in the storm...
We cant see the the stars that complete our
being

promises

When you fall apart again

I will hold your hands and show you the stars
And remind you that you too
Are made from the stars

I will remind you that your soul glows as
strongly as the stars
That you are
As *strong* as the stars

eyes

Your eyes are an infinite galaxy of stars
They hold each color of the world in a blend of
light and dark

So don't close your eyes
And hide away
The truths in your soul

infinte

I will love you
For infinity, until infinity.
Forever. And *Always*.

listen to me

Because your heart doesnt break everytime
someone hurts you,
Because even if you are crying, and you think
no one will be around to wipe them for you...

I will be there. To hold your heart in my hands.
To caress your cheek and to wipe your tears. I
will be there to remind you of the galaxy you
hold in your eyes and the stars that watch
upon you.

I won't lie. It will hurt. You will feel your skin
burn and blister. You will feel the ache in your
chest and the sting in your eyes when you cry.
But promise; Promise you won't ever stop
trying.

you

Cause darling,
You dont need to look any further
Than the person you see in the mirror

So *feel* the strength of the gravity that pulls
you down to earth
And heal your wounds with love
And remember to look,

and see the stars in your eyes,
 because they are, what make you shine